A DOZEN AND ONE
Pop Hits

Easy Piano Arrangements By JOHN BRIMHALL

Project Manager: Tony Esposito
Book Design: Michael Ramsay

© 1997 WARNER BROS. PUBLICATIONS
All Rights Reserved

CONTENTS

Plus Added Bonus Song! The Dance Sensation *Macarena*

From the Motion Picture "THE MIRROR HAS TWO FACES"

I FINALLY FOUND SOMEONE

Arranged by
JOHN BRIMHALL

Written by
BARBRA STREISAND, MARVIN HAMLISCH,
R. J. LANGE and BRYAN ADAMS

I Finally Found Someone - 6 - 1

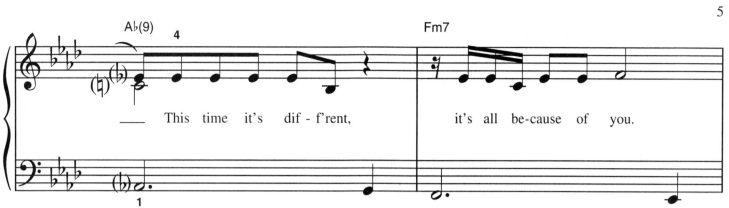

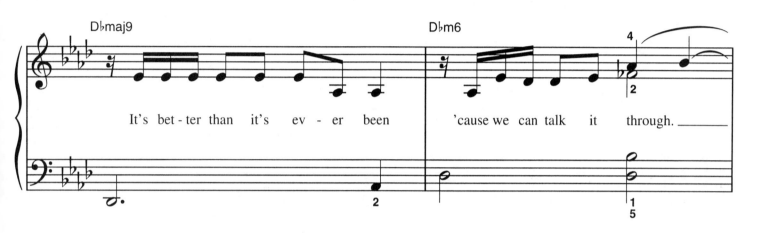

Chorus:

This is it! Oh, ___ I fi - n'lly found some - one, some -

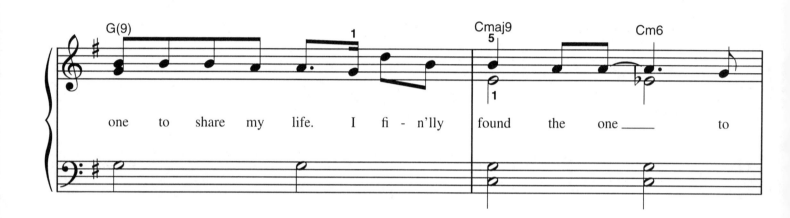

one to share my life. I fi - n'lly found the one ___ to

be with ev - 'ry ___ night. ___ 'Cause what - ev - er I do, ___ it's just

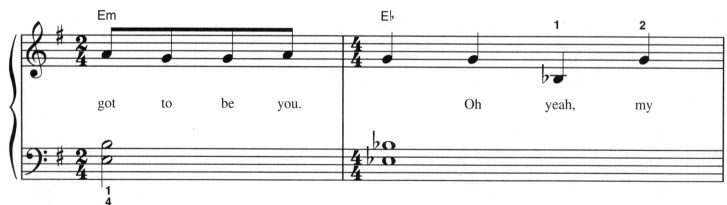

got to be you. Oh yeah, my

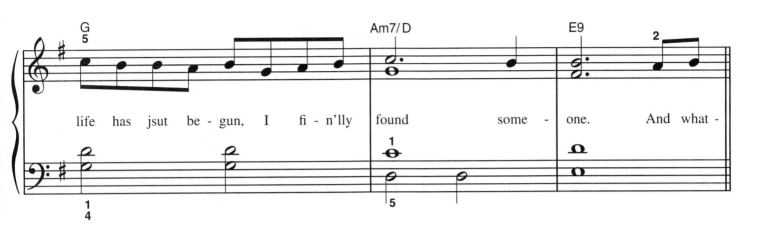

life has jsut be - gun, I fi - n'lly found some - one. And what -

ev - er I do, _____ it's just got to be you. Ooh, my

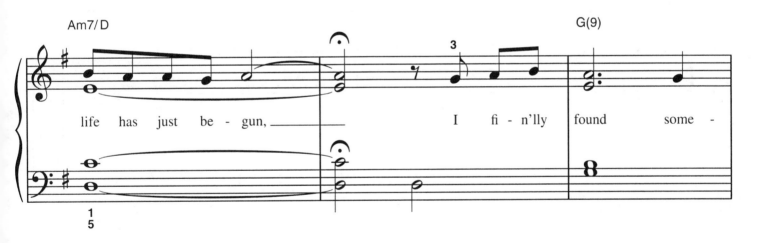

life has just be - gun, _____ I fi - n'lly found some -

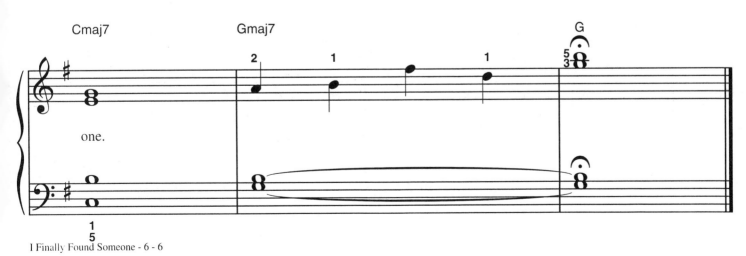

one.

CHANGE THE WORLD

Arranged by
JOHN BRIMHALL

Words and Music by
WAYNE KIRKPATRICK, TOMMY SIMS,
and GORDON KENNEDY

Moderately slow ♩ = 96

1. If I could reach the stars, I'd pull one down for
2. If I could be a king, e - ven for a

you, shine it on my heart
day, I'd take you as my queen.

so you could see the truth, that this love I have in -
I'd have it no oth - er way. And our love would

side is ev - ery - thing it seems.
rule in this king - dom we had made.

12

Change the World - 3 - 3

DESPERATELY WANTING

Arranged by
JOHN BRIMHALL

Words and Music by
KEVIN GRIFFIN

Desperately Wanting - 5 - 1

14

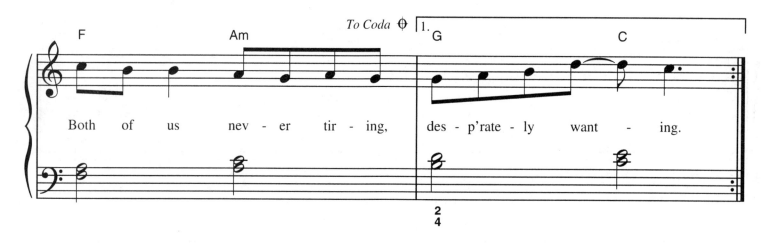

Both of us nev - er tir - ing, des - p'rate - ly want - ing.

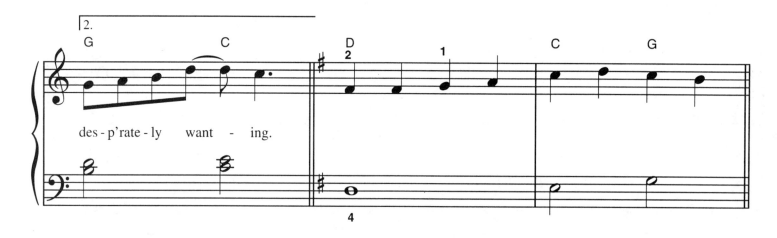

des - p'rate - ly want - ing.

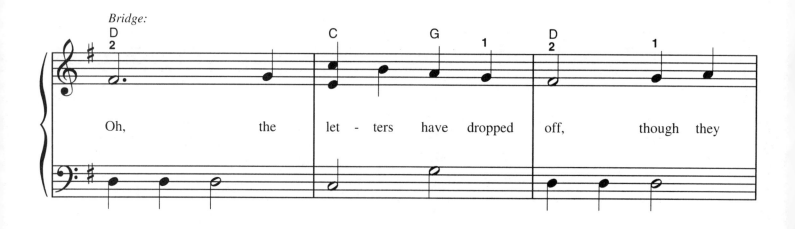

Bridge:

Oh, the let - ters have dropped off, though they

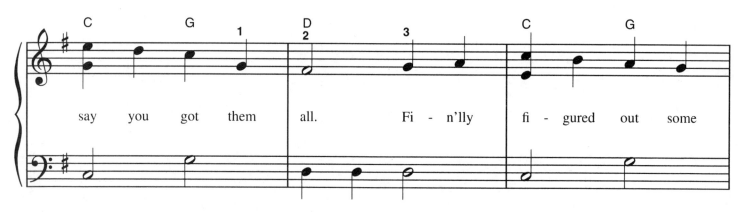

say you got them all. Fi - n'lly fi - gured out some

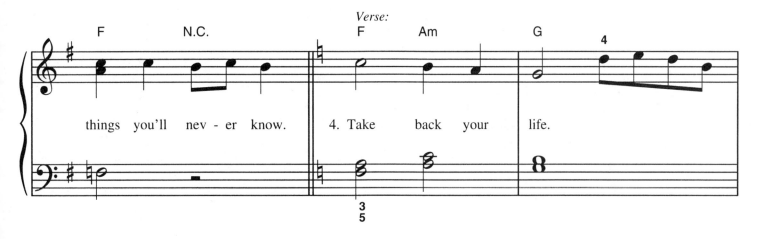

things you'll nev - er know.   4. Take   back   your   life.

Let   me   in - side.   We'll   find   the

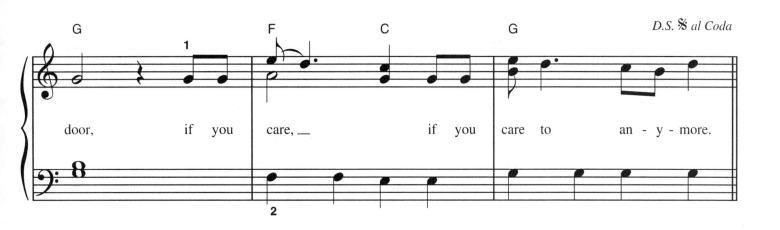

door,   if you   care, __   if   you   care to   an - y - more.

D.S. %️ al Coda

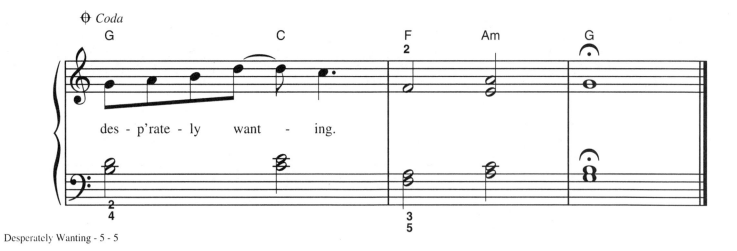

⊕ *Coda*

des - p'rate - ly   want - ing.

FAITHFULLY

Arranged by
JOHN BRIMHALL

Words and Music by
CHUCK JONES and PAM ROSE

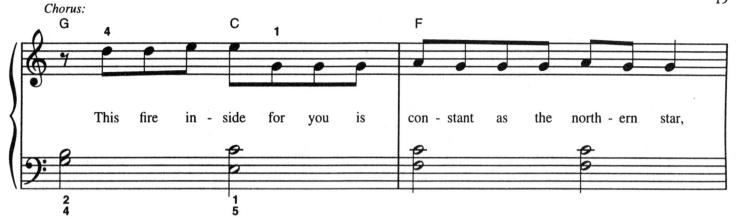

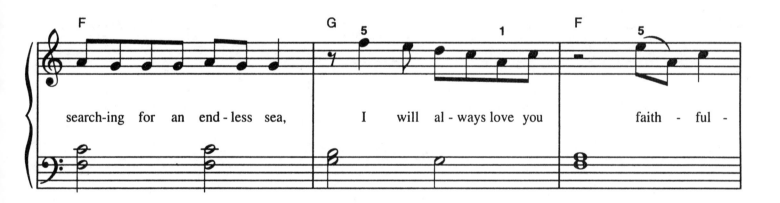

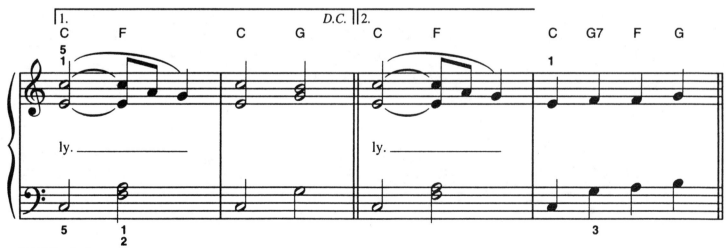

Chorus:

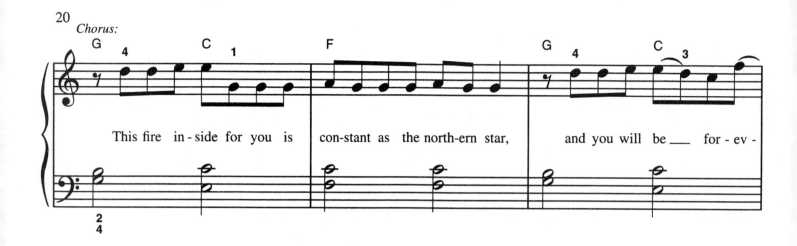

This fire in-side for you is con-stant as the north-ern star, and you will be ___ for - ev -

- er in my heart. As long as there's a riv - er search-ing for an end-less sea,

I will al - ways love you faith - ful - ly. _____

poco rit. e dim.

p

Faithfully - 3 - 3

FRIENDS

Arranged by
JOHN BRIMHALL

Words and Music by
JERRY HOLLAND

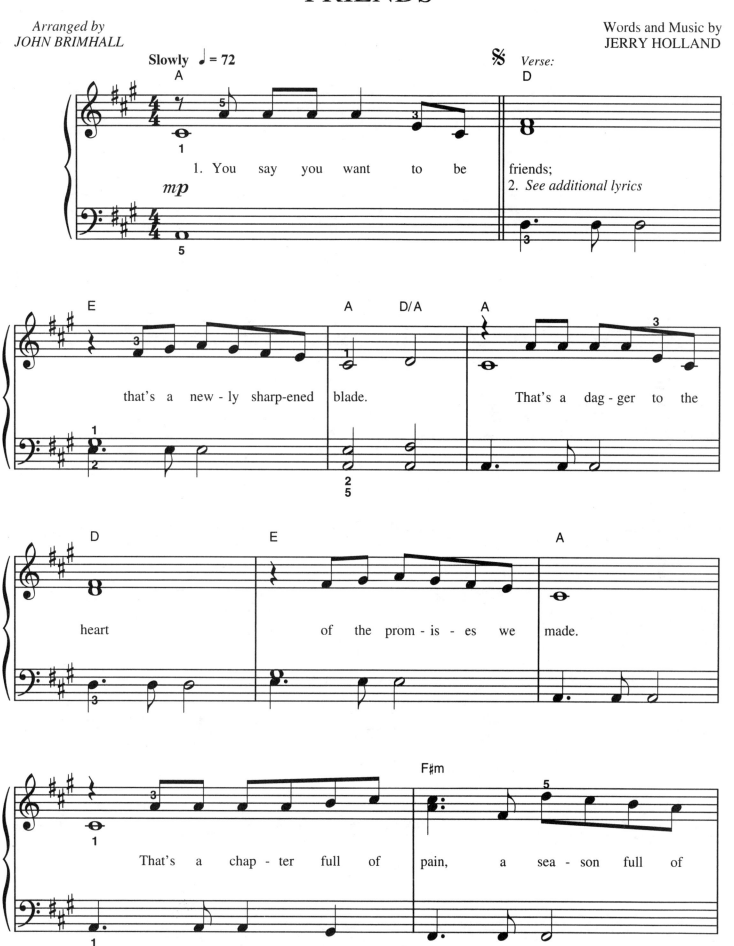

22

Friends - 3 - 2

Verse 2:
You say you love me very much,
And you'll always hold me dear.
Those are the sweetest words
I never want to hear.
What's a love without desire?
A flame without fire
Can't warm me late at night,
When I need you most.
(To Chorus:)

Friends - 3 - 3

From the Original Soundtrack Album "THE PREACHER'S WIFE"

I BELIEVE IN YOU AND ME

Arranged by
JOHN BRIMHALL

Words and Music by
SANDY LINZER and DAVID WOLFERT

I Believe in You and Me - 4 - 1

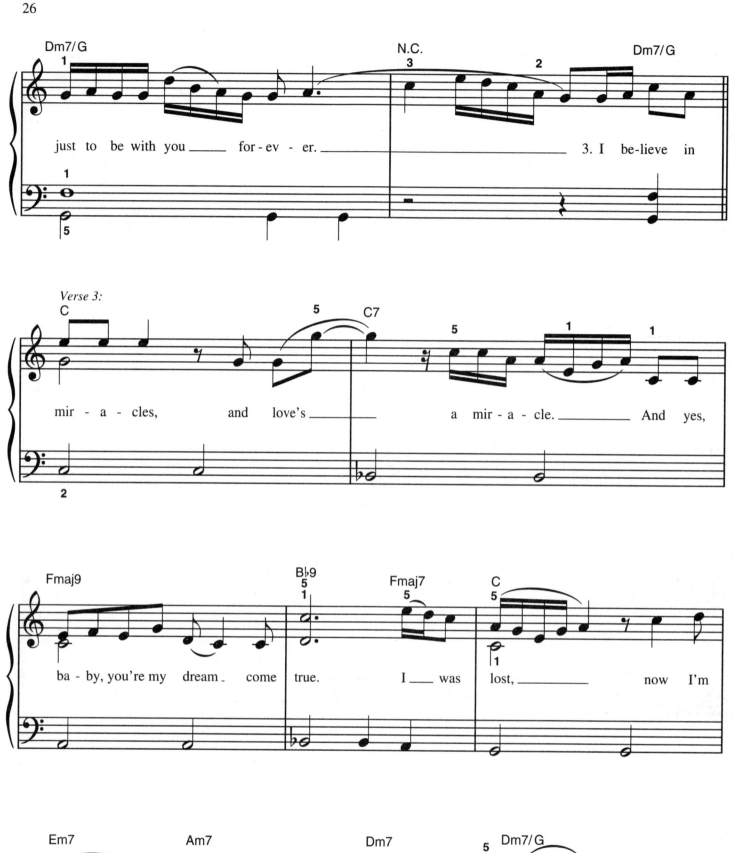

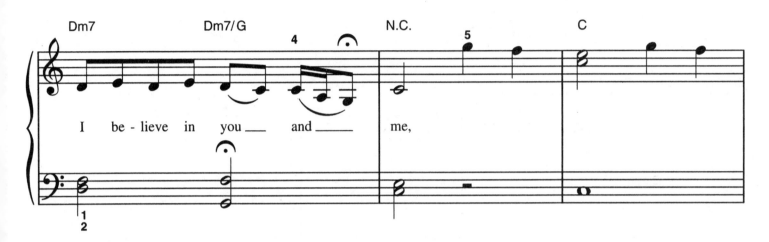

Verse 2:
I will never leave your side,
I will never hurt your pride.
When all the chips are down,
I will always be around,
Just to be right where you are, my love.
Oh, I love you, boy.
I will never leave you out,
I will always let you in
To places no one has ever been.
Deep inside, can't you see?
I believe in you and me.
(To Bridge:)

I BELIEVE I CAN FLY

Arranged by
JOHN BRIMHALL

Words and Music by
R. KELLY

I Believe I Can Fly - 3 - 1

30

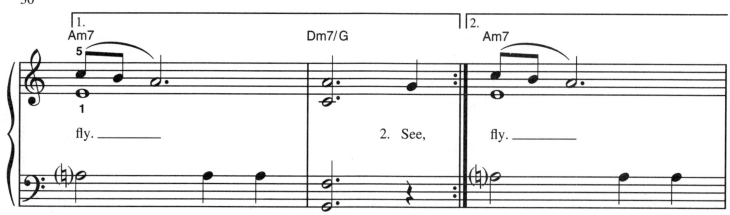

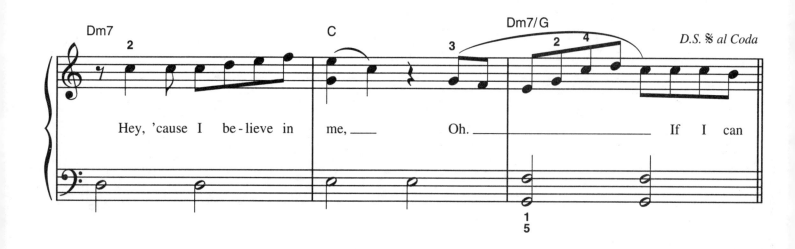

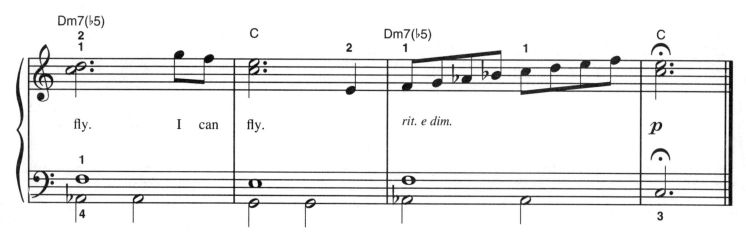

I Believe I Can Fly - 3 - 3

I'M NOT GIVING YOU UP

Arranged by
JOHN BRIMHALL

Words by
GLORIA ESTEFAN
Music by
KIKE SANTANDER

32

I'm Not Giving You up - 3 - 2

Verse 2:
Thinking back I see what we have is something different.
I think we've known all along.
So how fair would it be to divide this love's existence
Between what's right and what's wrong.
And you, always wond'ring if we'll make it.
Time will tell you that I'm not giving you up.
Oh, no, no, no.
(To Bridge:)

Verse 3:
Screaming in the silence the promises we've spoken
Come back to haunt me false and broken.
Quiet desperation to see we're lost forever,
Searching for water in this desert.
No, I refuse to have to do without your kisses.
I'm not giving you up, no, no.
(To Bridge:)

From the New Line Cinema Motion Picture "SET IT OFF"

DON'T LET GO (LOVE)

Arranged by
JOHN BRIMHALL

Words and Music by
ANDREA MARTIN, IVAN MATIAS,
MARQUEZE ETHERIDGE and ORGANIZED NOIZE

Don't Let Go (Love) - 4 - 1

Chorus:

Run - ning in and out my life _____ has got me so con -

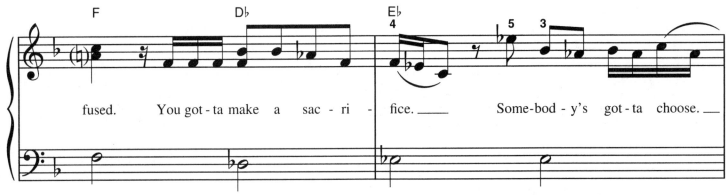

fused. You got - ta make a sac - ri - fice. _____ Some-bod - y's got - ta choose. __

_____ We can make it if we try _____ for the sake of you and

I. _____ To-geth-er we can make it right. _____ What's it gon - na

Verse 2:
I often fantasize the stars above are watching.
They know my heart,
How I speak to you is like only lovers do.
If I could wear your clothes,
I'd pretend I was you, and lose control, oh.

NOWHERE TO GO

Arranged by
JOHN BRIMHALL

Words and Music by
MELISSA ETHERIDGE

Moderately slow ♩ = 96

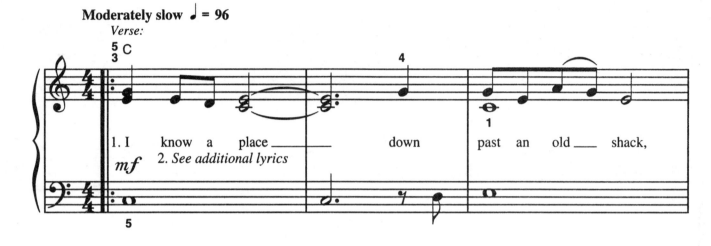

1. I know a place ____ down past an old ___ shack,
2. *See additional lyrics*

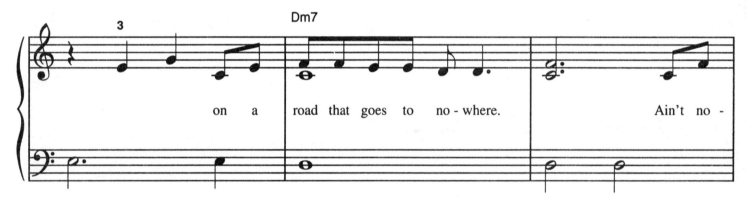

on a road that goes to no - where. Ain't no -

bod - y com-ing back. We can go ___ there to - night, ___ we can

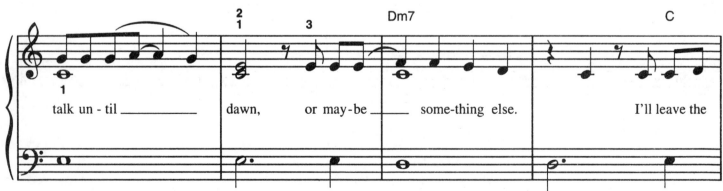

talk un - til _____ dawn, or may-be ___ some-thing else. I'll leave the

Nowhere to Go - 3 - 1

Verse 2:
Past the Walmart and the prison, down by the old V.A.
Just my jeans and my T shirt, and my blue Chevrolet.
It's Saturday night, feels like everything's wrong.
I've got some strawberry wine,
I want to get you alone, get you alone.

Verse 3:
Down by the muddy water of the mighty Mo,
In an old abandoned boxcar, will I ever know?
Dance with me forever, this moment is divine.
I'm so close to heaven,
This hell is not mine, this hell is not mine.

UN-BREAK MY HEART

Arranged by
JOHN BRIMHALL

Words and Music by
DIANE WARREN

42

YOU WERE MEANT FOR ME

Arranged by
JOHN BRIMHALL

Words and Music by
JEWEL KILCHER and STEVE POLTZ

1. I hear the clock, it's six A. M. ___
2.3. *See additional lyrics*

I feel so far ___ from where I've been. I've got my eggs and my

pan - cakes, too, ___ I've got ma - ple syr - up, ev - 'ry-

thing but you. ___ I break the yolks and make a smil - y face, ___

You Were Meant for Me - 4 - 2

46

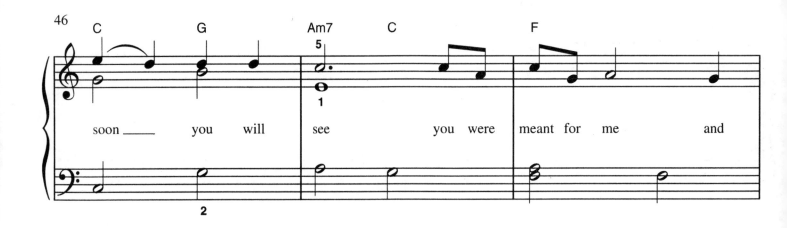

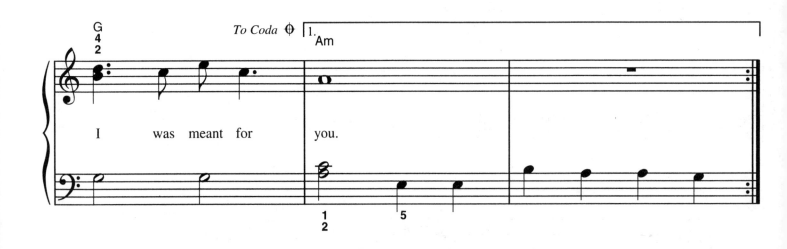

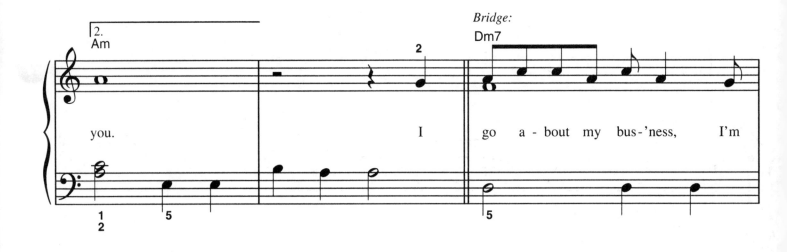

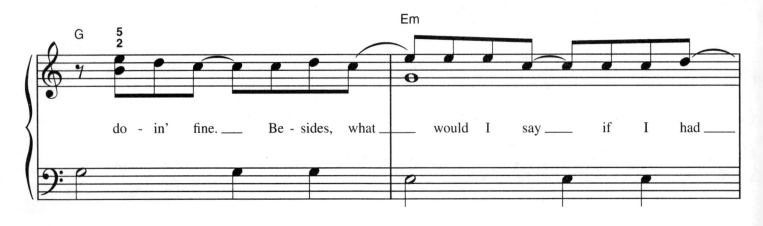

You Were Meant for Me - 4 - 3

Verse 2:
I called my mama, she was out for a walk.
Consoled a cup of coffee, but it didn't wanna talk.
So I picked up a paper, it was more bad news,
More hearts being broken or people being used.
Put on my coat in the pouring rain.
I saw a movie, it just wasn't the same,
'Cause it was happy and I was sad,
And it made me miss you, oh, so bad.
(To Chorus:)

Verse 3:
I brush my teeth and put the cap back on,
I know you hate it when I leave the light on.
I pick a book up and then I turn the sheets down,
And then I take a breath and a good look around.
Put on my pj's and hop into bed.
I'm half alive but I feel mostly dead.
I try and tell myself it'll be all right,
I just shouldn't think anymore tonight.
(To Chorus:)

IF IT MAKES YOU HAPPY

Arranged by
JOHN BRIMHALL

Words and Music by
SHERYL CROW and JEFF TROTT

If You Makes You Happy - 4 - 1

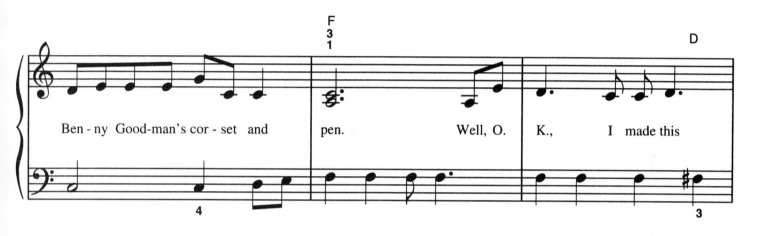

Chorus:

If You Makes You Happy - 4 - 2

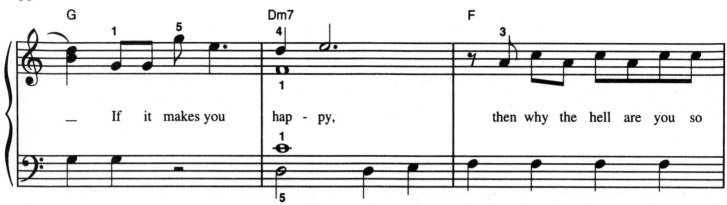

If it makes you hap - py, then why the hell are you so

sad? 2. You get sad?

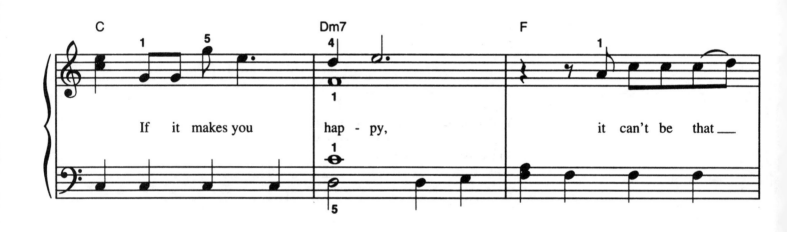

If it makes you hap - py, it can't be that

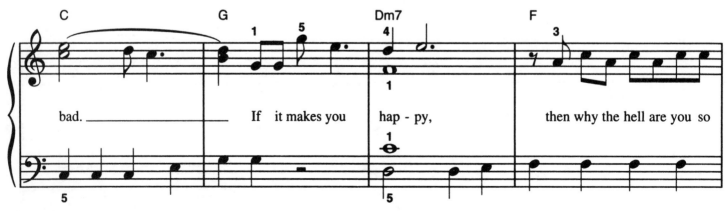

bad. _____ If it makes you hap - py, then why the hell are you so

sad?

3. We've been

sad?

Verse 2:
You get down, real low down.
You listen to Coltrane,
Derail your own train.
Well, who hasn't been there before?
I come 'round, around the hard way.
Bring you comics in bed,
Scrape the mold off the bread,
And serve you french toast again.
Well, O.K., I still get stoned.
I'm not the kind of girl you'd take home.

Chorus:
If it makes you happy,
It can't be that bad.
If it makes you happy,
Then why the hell are you so sad?

Verse 3:
We've been so far, far away from here.
Put on a poncho, played for mosquitos,
And everywhere in between.
Well, O.K., we get along.
So what if right now everything's wrong?
(To Chorus:)

MACARENA

Arranged by
JOHN BRIMHALL

Words and Music by
ANTONIO ROMERO and RAFAEL RUIZ

Dance rock ♩ = 112

Macarena - 3 - 1

Coro:
Dale a tu cuerpo alegría Macarena
Que tu cuerpo es pa' darle alegría y cosa buena.
Dale a tu cuerpo alegría Macarena, eh, Macarena.

Dale a tu cuerpo alegría Macarena
Que tu cuerpo es pa' darle alegría y cosa buena.
Dale a tu cuerpo alegría Macarena, eh, Macarena.

Verso 1:
Macarena tiene un novio que se llama,
Que se llama de apellido Vitorino.
Y en la jura de bandera del muchacho
Se la dió con dos amigos.

Puente 1:
Macarena tiene un novio que se llama,
Que se llama de apellido Vitorino.
Y en la jura de bandera del muchacho
Se la dió con dos amigos.
(Al Coro:)

Verso 2:
Macarena, Macarena, Macarena,
Que te gustan los veranos de Marbelia.
Macarena, Macarena, Macarena,
Que te gusto la movida guerrillera.
(Al Coro:)

Verso 3:
Macarena sueña con el Corte inglés
Y se compra los modelos mas modernos.
Le gustaría vivir en Nueva York
Y ligar un novio nuevo.

Puente 2:
Macarena sueña con el Corte inglés
Y se compra los modelos mas modernos.
Le gustaría vivir en Nueva York
Y ligar un novio nuevo.
(Al Coro:)

Verso 4:
Macarena tiene un novio que se llama,
Que se llama de apellido Vitorino.
Y en la jura de bandera del muchacho
Se la dió con dos amigos.

Puente 3:
Macarena tiene un novio que se llama,
Que se llama de apellido Vitorino.
Y en la jura de bandera del muchacho
Se la dió con dos amigos.
(Al Coro:)

John Brimhall's
LEISURE TIME
PIANO

67 Popular Easy Piano Pieces

These books feature teaching aids such as fingerings and a key signature index. Appropriate for very easy to intermediate levels. Spice up that piano lesson!

67 Country Easy Piano Pieces (TEP0133)

Includes: The Dance ● Elvira ● Forever's as Far as I'll Go ● Hey, Good Lookin' ● I Will Always Love You ● Tennessee Waltz ● When Will I Be Loved.

67 Popular Easy Piano Pieces (TEP0121C)

Includes: The Best Is Yet to Come ● Don't Blame Me ● Linus and Lucy ● Out of Nowhere ● The Pink Panther ● Theme from Ice Castles (Through the Eyes of Love) ● Up Where We Belong.

67 More Popular Easy Piano Pieces (TEP0122C)

Titles include: Don't Cry Out Loud ● I Love a Rainy Night ● It's the Most Wonderful Time of the Year ● The Most Beautiful Girl ● Once Upon a Time ● Tangerine.

Another 67 Popular Easy Piano Pieces (TEP0127)

Includes: After All (Love Theme from *Chances Are)* ● Anything for You ● California Girls ● Crying ● Don't Get Around Much Anymore ● For Once in My Life ● Here and Now ● Let the River Run (New Jerusalem) (Theme from *Working Girl)* ● Put on a Happy Face ● You and I.

Today's Easy Adult Piano

Easy piano arrangements of hit popular songs and important popular standards, designed for adults and teenagers. The arrangements are at a 2nd and 3rd year level, depending on the complexity of the songs themselves.

Book 1 (TEP0102B)

17 titles including: From a Distance ● Heart and Soul ● Love Theme from St. Elmo's Fire ● Old Time Rock & Roll ● You're the Inspiration.

Book 2 (TEP0126)

16 titles like: Anything for You ● Here and Now ● Here We Are ● Oh, Pretty Woman ● Travelin' Man ● The Vows Go Unbroken (Always True to You).

All-Time Favorites (TEP0128)

22 titles including: Alexander's Ragtime Band ● Baby Face ● Blue Moon ● Bye Bye Blackbird ● I'm Looking Over a Four-Leaf Clover ● Oh, You Beautiful Doll ● Stormy Weather (Keeps Rainin' All the Time).

The Broadway Book (TEP0107)

16 titles, including Big Spender ● If My Friends Could See Me Now ● Send in the Clowns.

The Country Book (TEP0108)

17 titles, including City of New Orleans ● Don't It Make My Brown Eyes Blue ● The Gambler ● Stand by Your Man.

The Jazz Book (TEP0125)

19 titles, including Don't Get Around Much Anymore ● On the Sunny Side of the Street ● Satin Doll.

The Motown Book (TEP0129)

16 movin' classics like: Ain't No Mountain High Enough ● Heat Wave (Love Is Like a Heat Wave) ● I Heard It Through the Grapevine ● Stop! In the Name of Love ● The Tracks of My Tears ● You Are the Sunshine of My Life.

Pops, Book 3 (TEP0132)

These 18 arrangements are especially noted for their playability and the true character of each song is maintained. Includes: Always ● The Dance ● (Everything I Do) I Do It for You ● From a Distance ● Linus and Lucy ● More Than Words ● The Pink Panther.

The Rock 'N' Roll Book (TEP0124)

21 titles: '50s and '60s: Splish Splash ● Johnny Angel ● Oh, Pretty Woman ● (We're Gonna) Rock Around the Clock.

33 Popular Duets For Easy Piano

33 great duets in each convenient, spiral-bound collection. A wonderful variety of popular hits, standards, classics, hymns and Christmas favorites. Great for lessons or just for fun.

33 Popular Duets (TPD0023)

Titles include: The Church in the Wildwood ● Colour My World ● Dance of the Sugar Plum Fairy ● Lara's Theme ● Over the Rainbow ● Tales from the Vienna Woods ● We Wish You a Merry Christmas.

33 More Popular Duets (TPD0024)

Includes: Amazing Grace ● I'd Like to Teach the World to Sing ● Miss You Like Crazy ● Toreador Song (from *Carmen)* ● Silver Bells ● Raindrops Keep Falling on My Head ● Moon River.

JOHN BRIMHALL

Easy Piano Arrangements of...

Our newly published Composer Series features the biggest hits by some of the greatest songwriters that have ever lived. This series, containing perfectly set Easy Piano arrangements by John Brimhall, is very accessible and is sure to please students, teachers, and anyone else interested in classic, well-written songs. Not only are the arrangements pleasing to the ear and lie nicely under the hands, they also demonstrate John Brimhall's special ability to capture the subtle nuances and harmonies of each song. These timeless songs will bring pianists back to these folios again and again!

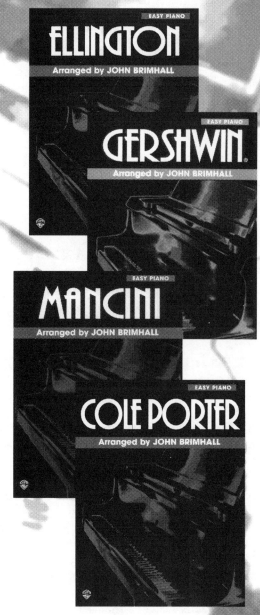

ELLINGTON
arranged by John Brimhall
____ (AF9619) Easy Piano
Twenty-two standards from Edward "Duke" Ellington, the most important composer of the big band era, are collected here. Titles include: Sophisticated Lady • I Got It Bad (And That Ain't Good) • Mood Indigo • Take the "A" Train • It Don't Mean a Thing (If It Ain't Got That Swing) • Don't Get Around Much Anymore • Caravan and many more.

GERSHWIN®
arranged by John Brimhall
____ (AF9561) Easy Piano
Within this fabulous collection, 26 songs have been exquisitely and perfectly set at the easy piano level by John Brimhall. Titles include: Bess, You Is My Woman • Embraceable You • (A) Foggy Day • I Got Rhythm • Liza • Oh, Lady Be Good • Someone to Watch Over Me • Summertime • 'S Wonderful • They All Laughed and other Gershwin greats.

MANCINI
arranged by John Brimhall
____ (AF9617) Easy Piano
Henry Mancini is considered the foremost composer of film and television themes. This 26-song folio contains his most memorable songs, including: Peter Gunn • Pink Panther • Days of Wine and Roses • Moon River • Two for the Road • Breakfast at Tiffany's • Mr. Lucky • Baby Elephant Walk and more.

COLE PORTER
arranged by John Brimhall
____ (AF9667) Easy Piano
Over 20 titles have been collected in this fabulous folio, including: All of You • Anything Goes • Begin the Beguine • I Get a Kick Out of You • I Love You • In the Still of the Night • I've Got You Under My Skin • Just One of Those Things • Let's Do It • Night and Day • So in Love • True Love • You Do Something to Me and many other classics from Cole Porter.